C000103003

**the flap pamphlet series**

# *Pigeon Party*

Anita.
Remember – you are
beautiful. Thank you
for everything you
uncovered
in me.
for home for Debris.

**⏣flap**

*open, read, turn*

## Pigeon Party
the flap pamphlet series (No. 11)
Printed and Bound in the United Kingdom

Published by the flap series, 2014
the pamphlet series of flipped eye publishing
All Rights Reserved

Cover Design by Petraski
Series Design © flipped eye publishing, 2010

**Acknowledgements:**
*For listening:* Joêl Daniel.
*For Teaching:* Jacob Sam-La Rose, Peter Kahn, Charlie Dark, Cathy
Grindrod, Nicola Valentine, Kayo Chingonyi, Patricia Smith, Terrance
Hayes, Seamus Heaney, Nottingham University, Writing East Midlands
and YearDot.
*For Creating:* Lydia, Paul, Gary and Richard Stevenson.
*For Caring:* Anne Holloway, Ioney Smallhorne, Bea Udeh, Suzie-Lea
Coltham, Mika Curtis, Jessiman Landy, Millz and Pabz.
*And for my Career:* Each and every Mouthy Poet.

With thanks to Bohdan Piasecki and Apples & Snakes for funding my
mentorship from Niall O'Sullivan, my editor.

ISBN-13: 978-1-905233-45-8
*Editorial work for this series is supported by the Arts Council of England*

**LOTTERY FUNDED**

# Pigeon Party

Debris Stevenson

# What they say about Debris

"If only the year 9s could meet people like Debris, then they'd all love English!" – A Year 8, *Nottingham University Samworth Academy*

"What I search for, more so than performance technique or even simple stage presence and charisma is great text, well written, well-structured and suited to the subject matter. Deborah Stevenson was born with a captivating stage presence and her charisma precedes her years, but both of those qualities are humbled, even dwarfed, by her gift with the pen." – Inua Ellams

"One of the brightest young voices of literature to emerge from our shores in over two decades. A powerful performer and an excellent writer whose poems evoke emotion and mood with every word. Wise beyond her years, articulate, intelligent and polite, Deborah is poised to help drag the spoken word movement out of the dark ages. A testament to the importance of teaching poetry in schools." – Charlie Dark

# Contents | *Pigeon Party*

*"There they are.*
*Thirty at the corner.*
*Black, raw, ready.*
*Sores in the city*
*that do not want to heal."*

**The Blackstone Rangers** by Gwendolyn Brooks.


# After The Blackstone Rangers
## i. Cecil Park – High as the Swings


They were teaching me how to roll up. There,
on the swings, everyone was learning. They
were grey Pitbulls going for an un-bagged shit. "Are
we drinking enough?" One asks, as thirty
sheets of Rizla angel from my fingers. The wind at
1am, weed rolled loose as a Tesco bag, the
polystyrene cup cracked under our teeth. In the corner

sharing headphones, listening to Dizzee's black
vibrations, backs of our heads touching. Raw
rum laughing. As our throats throb ready
smoke. Sitting on the swings, the 8 year old sores
scabbed and pickable, worth the scars set in
memories that fit on fingers like Hoola-Hoops. The
lighters set fire to bins for warmth and jokes. The city –
a shitty sun. We've needed a new one for a while – that
doesn't soak into the tarmac like chewing gum. Do

we feel cold? Our skin does but our minds do not...
like scotch bonnets. I ask, "Is this what we want?"
They walk their swings to tip toe. Jump-ready. Aiming to
the suspicious sun. We'd do anything. Anything, to heal.

# Disposable and Warm

*A festival fling comes to an end.*

My two man Teflon smells of Sambuca.
We slot its spine together. Giggle legs
against each other. A silent disco's
inside our mouths. A barbecue's our chests.
You beckon freedom like a bouncy ball.
We run. You bundle into a ball pit.
Pull my waist in with you. Let our weight fall.
Our voices collide like torch-lights outside.

I crack our can of Scrumpy Jacks. Our fun
still disposable and warm. I wait for
a wriggling softness. Moist – a shell-shaped head
between us. As you sleep, closed and fragile,
my throat remembers play and smacks
the vomit, like ash, from my back.

# In Some Ways

Her Dad lies unconscious beneath
the Christmas tree. She palms away glass,
crushes lines of coke from the coffee table
into a lunch-box. Squeezes milk into a pan.

Nudges the kettle. Sometimes I come over
on Boxing Day, drink mulled wine, eat gammon.
Steak knives are the only form of cutlery;
for stirring full-fat milk into tea.

When she comes over my house,
my parents get angry, say she drinks
all the orange juice, goes to the toilet
with the door open and doesn't wash her hands.

Their accusations are true, in some ways.

## Quality Street

Small metal buckets filled with chips proper.
Hot and English. Windy cheese and onion cobs
sea-wet and salt-dry. Tinned mushy pea sky,
seagulls move the tide like prayer.
Our tongues chase melting vanilla.
Forgetting about Christmas or holiday pay.
We fight for the right vinegar,
blow the steam from wooden fork wishes.

We struggle over the orange and pink Quality Street.
Whilst Mum and Dad, one cod, one kipper, sit
on the pier, touch knees, tear open sachets
and eat quickly for fear of sand.

The seagulls see pick-nick families –
unhappy and hungry. One drives down
takes the batter, wooden fork, and sandwiched knees
with the last cod in the shop, from Dad's pile of newspaper

and cheese, firmly in distancing beak.

We take cover, crouch under hands and white plastic tables,
watch through telescope gaps in fingers
as Mum eats her kipper like a kiss
and Dad licks onion vinegar, laughing, from his fist.

# Dean Charles Biting a Girl's Ear Off on the 86 Bus Home from School

He swelters above her
as schools of patterned tights and ties
rise from the multi-coloured seats.

"BEEF, BEEF, BEEF, BEEF!"
Chips confetti round the isle:
ketchup, vinegar, grease.

Capital letter stamped caps
squeeze into the rave of bodies.
Camera phones slap the ceiling happy.

We want to see something.
Wait. Watch the wet of her skin.
Heavy with breath, she bobs like an apple,

a bucket of water beneath him.
Wait. He laces the fruit of her face
across the top deck. Her lips

pop like a paint-filled balloon.
We thought we wanted the best view.
His eyes wishing low

over her cheeks glow.
He wraps his teeth

around her balance,
tugs gently and spits.

# Counselling

Spit in a watering can until it is full. Call up your mum and tell her what you did. Tell her it is a metaphor for something, something involving her. Let her guess. Rip all the sleeves off your shirts. Call up your dad. Tell him what you did. Tell him your arms are cold. Ask him if he has a solution. Wait.

# Nonna

*For my Mum & Dad, and their own.*

I lay my hand wide across her face.
It is expensive and dark as a roof slate.
There are fat puddles under her eyes,
shiny with reflections and feet.

Still bath water. Warm.
I run my finger over the film
where air and liquid meet. Hair and blood
thinning. She feels loose as an eyelash.

They kept her wired and warm for me.
For my hands not yet half the size of her head.
They kept her wired and warm for me.
My understanding not yet half the size of her death.

# Should You Raise Him in the 'Hood'?

My first son will have dreadlocks
the shade of wheat sheaves –
stockier than his school blazer
by the time he is fourteen.

He has to heap and wrap them:
wicker on his head, to wave arms like
scotch bonnet, Trench Town and bloodfire
in an under-18's night, Oceana.

He suns space where there are clouds of body,
has perfectly kissed teeth and air flares
in his speech. I open the passenger door,
my face outstretched with sugar cane.

He's sober until we get home. Where
he leaves the bathroom full with shea butter
and towels soaked in hip-hop. He sleeps.
The hallway smells of Curry Goat for Sunday.

He has his father's speed in his mouth,
yellow ackee in his skin and rebellion
in his school reports. I wonder what
the absence has done. Turn on the TV for sleep –

a documentary on Michael Johnson's legs
suggests my mama's Jamaica
was a Slave Referral Unit, after uncool
Africans had been bred thick, strong

and long as boats and trees.
Steel to stretch lick and rip.
The green eyes of rape.

The silence of homophobic buggery
and a smile with the statement, "they'd kill you
for that in my country." In the morning,

he will watch this documentary,
as he bites hot sauce from his nails,
Mama tightening RedRat into his locks
after Bible practice. We will break laughter

as I remind him of Jamaica's white shoes,
stretch marks of silver and the confidence to deliver
even when they can't. It's understanding
of my body: violently polite, just like his

report card. Like all the things we'll forget
to tell each other about Oceana, or our history
and Our Father. I'll think of our hands
holding a knife to a boned leg of meat,

the scent of hair grease
and the dilation of our bodies to
ghetto-blasting dark cloudy music.
Red Stripe shandy kissing our teeth

and garden moonlight
bright as wheat sheaves
wrapped like the arms of a child
around my head.

# Love Poem

You vomited on my skirt.
You told your mum they were my cigarettes.
You tell me my boyfriend, Patrick, is a pussy.

But you harboured me and my brother for months through the divorce.
You came to Bristol, Edinburgh, Norwich, wherever I'd perform.
You furnished hot Hennessy and lemon, rang to claim nothing,
when the world aborted me.

And everyone's saying I should hit you.

Everyone says I should hit you –
but we're parallel in Victoria Park's public loos,
near the swings we used to queue to get to,
and you are being
sick on my skirt

because they accidentally gave you too much
anaesthetic in the termination.

I gag my jumper around your thighs
before you can understand the blood,
tell you it's cold,

don't tell you I know the baby
was my pussy of a boyfriend's.

Syringe-like voices scream
I should swing for you

I still don't know if I will.
For now I cradle your hair
and direct your head to the toilet.

# Bread Machine Teen

*On overhearing a schoolgirls phone conversation on the 25 bus.*

I want a more African bottom.
That's what's missing.
A batty a baby could be propped up on.

I want lots actually...
Naked raving torsos in conga lines.
Peeing without touching the toilet seat.

Sweat patches everywhere,
the smell of everyone's.
The drop: dancing mid-air

until my trousers split
like embarrassment does
in the presence of skin music.

The nudity my dreams tried to scare you out of.
The jumper my best mate lent me
to cover the hole

so I could keep moving my hips
like a bread machine.

# Recipe

Not all ceviche is created equal.
You need the freshest raw fish,
just enough Peruvian lime,
a chilli ground.
Sea salt.

The methods and timings
swell the fish with acidity
like our first time in Jesus Maria market, Lima,
the smell of quick hands trading hot herbs
and raw fish waiting to turn like litmus paper.

Waiting to turn
like inspiration
like a dinner party
like the backs of our hands touching
like your voice flickering to apologies
like a waiter who thought we said medium
when we wanted rare.

*Partially Found Poem from Ceviche Recipe at http://cevicheuk.com/*

# Power Dynamic of Slags and Virgins in East London

*"I walk naked under my clothes like anyone else,*
*and I'm not a bomb to explode in your hands."*
(Dramatic Monologue in the Speakers Voice,
Vassar Miller. 1991)


She had morals for ladders in her tights, whilst I
had a hymen, still do. So she pissed me off. We'd walk
the same route home. Her slimy naked
pride – strawberries out of season and hidden under
her blazer from the corner shop. Her smiles were oral. My
eyes were blue, skin sunned beige which made my clothes
riper. Her clothes were cucumber tutorials,         like
the videos everyone finds too funny to watch.      Anyone
could guess at life like she did. So I wouldn't dare,        or else
I'd be as bad, right? I stole her seat in the dinner hall once and
cut open her school-bag. Left her, on knees – gathering.   I'm
regretting it now of course. Now I understand sex is not
            introduced to us all in the same way. A
                    hymen can be a bomb
a means of terrorism inside. To
be hidden in an allotment and tampered with until it explodes.
I don't remember anything of hers. Just that her name was Francesca. In
her cleavage was a tattoo of Betty Boop and her name. You're
just as bad as her I guess, if you can only see the bomb in her hands.

# On Parliament Street

*With thanks to Caroline Bird.*

The men who prey upon the vulnerable women
at AA meetings are nick-named "pigeon-fuckers."
Clive, top pigeon-fucker, has hands like sycamore tree.
These women haven't seen trees in daylight.

Clive starts each meeting with a coffee and an Oreo,
his mouth finding new ways to peel out the centre.
Sharon, Viv and Marilyn watch from the bulge
of their glass livers. He sets personal goals.

Sharon in the stationary cupboard
hugging a ruler inside her, in return
for a clean shot of urine the next week.

On Saturday mornings he suckles Viv dizzy,
her mind bloodless and swirled,
her womb too nostalgic for fear.

Marilyn likes her motivation simple:
"post-session shags" with treacle.
Punctuality has never been so high.

His hands are seeds,
body a bird-bath in Victoria Park,
covered in shit and Pro Plus,

his voice an examiner,
a timer, a pregnancy test,
a hallucinogen convinced of flight.

His mouth; a mudguard,
the fat drains of London,
a lip, a belt, a frog.

These women,
all glass and feather,
who call for him.

# Named

I found a spade in the bed
instead of your body

it was Simoned in slime:
the traces of pond from out back.

The house smelt of Aaron and Ash.
The woolen soles of your slippers

dredged across the kitchen.
He'd never Joshed us over like this before…

My chest was hot with Honey
and raw-milk. The phone's ring was Jerening

through my hips.
He hadn't closed the curtains.

He hadn't Petered the fridge.
The crush of your cry

couldn't leave
a Jim or a Sacha.

I can tell he attempted
to fill the bath with Daniel.

The steam still hovered

under the door, into the front garden

where your nameless
fat limbs lay.

Willow branches cast shadows,
fingers miming the wings of a crow

and the head of a dog
and other things
with names.

# Ground Zero

Vinnie sets the pigeon alight.
A litre of straight Smirnoff tightens around her wings,
melts the curtains. Six-pack rings around her body.
The block's altitude drains police siren hurricanes
as her heat palpitates and spits. Burns my irises. The floor
is black. The fire like metal in a microwave. And I watch.

Vinnie rolls up a collage of Rizla… and I watch
his cocoon of fist. He flicks on my lighter.
Chucks it back empty. Cheeky. The floor
is smoking with us, its scent camouflaging her wings.
Blood stains dry like worn varnish. She's a hurricane
fading into history: another famous, bodiless

female name. On the walls, unnaturally bottomed bodies
are held in pound shop posters. Vinnie takes off his ToyWatch,
crucifix and earring. Like a Texan awaiting a hurricane,
he blacks out the windows. Eyes still like club night lights.
Cupboards flake chipboard. The MDF wings
of a cannabis leaf, spray painted purple on the floor.

It's Monday. My red eyelids feel like floorboards.
I wonder… on Ley Street, how many other somebodies
feel like this? Concrete gardens covered in winged

27

rats and rats, always a skirting board away. I watch
one paperboy. Peddling for penny sweets he'll sell for five. Bike lights
beaming. He turns his paper round and round. Makes his own hurricanes.

He must know every street name and has taught his feet to hurricane
over broken basketball courts then back to Choco Puffs and fake floorboards.
Still managing to jump over the back gate in time... Vinnie bought his first lighter
with cherry sherbet profits, kicked upside down by somebody
kidnapping the contents of his pockets: the lighter, keys and his mum's watch.
Cumulonimbus formed a hood over Vinnie's good looks. With wings

made of a post-prison thickness, bench-pressed on chicken wings.
When Vinnie and me quit stabilizers, we reclined in the eye of the hurricane.
People claim it's calm there. It's terrifying. Watching
pitpulls, Halal Fried Chicken Shops, padded pants and floor
tiles revolve like vultures or one dirty gray dove just as terrified as us. Her body
reflecting, like Vinnie, the nudist nature of sunlight

at 8am. When school startles Siamese houses to flap wings against daylight.
From The Iron Bridge, I watch blazers, backpacks, bodies follow me.
Fluffy hurricanes flip out the nest. Aim for the patch of grass on the ground-floor.

*"Hardly Belafonte, King,*
*Black Jesus, Stokely, Malcolm X or Rap.*
*Bungled trophies.*
*Their country is a nation on no map."*

**The Blackstone Rangers** by Gwendolyn Brooks.

# After The Blackstone Rangers
## ii. Dutch Pot Dancing

In the back of a Dutch Pot shop, 200 sweating bodies hardly
smell of anything. It's a happy stink. We're Belafonte
banana boats inventing Calypso with motions. Kings
of testosterone. We pack in until even the air is Black.
Hair new and waxed. We are happy being 16, as Jesus
might have been. Singing "follow the leader." Leaders, Stokely,
presidents of panther mentality, beautiful as violent Malcolm
when he was real-life-living, before the power of X.

Pelvises kissing. I haven't drunk or smoked a thing or
had time to decide if I want to. Hips learning flow like rap.
Little boys learn to hold bigger girls. Heads bungled
into pink lace front wigs, passing out plastic punch cup trophies,
smells of bass, tastes of steamed up windows. Synchronised. Their
feet drawing patterns like 8-year-old fingers from car seats. A country
made of multi-coloured beats. Fenugreek and clove over meat is
sometimes enough for peace and a party. Enough for me to be a
dancehall queen. Enough for all of us to taste at home in a nation
where statistics can only expose a cocktail-stick. I lead the chants on
"Trinidad… follow the leader… raise ya' hand… love and unity." No
one can shout louder. But everyone can add a new move to our map.

Lightning Source UK Ltd.
Milton Keynes UK
UKOW03f1241140514

231676UK00002B/18/P